Warfare in a High-Tech Age

Sally and Adrian Morgan

Heinemann
LIBRARY
Chicago, Illinois

Customer Service 888-454-2279

Visit our website at www.heinemannlibrary.com

Illustrations by Barry Atkinson and Jeff Edwards
Originated by Repro Multi Warna
Printed and bound in China by SCPC Company Limited

10 09 08 07
10 9 8 7 6 5 4 3 2 1

Library of Congress Cataloging-in-Publication Data
Morgan, Adrian; Morgan, Sally
    Warfare in a hi-tech age / Sally and Adrian Morgan.
        p. cm. -- (Science at the edge)
    Includes index.
    ISBN 13: 978-1-4034-7765-1 (library binding - hardcover)
    ISBN 13: 978-1-4034-9129-9 (paperback)
    1. Military art and science--History--21st century--Juvenile literature.
    2. Military weapons--History--21st century--Juvenile literature.   I. Morgan, Adrian.
    II. Title. III. Series.
    U42.M68 2005
    355.02--dc22
                                                    2005024171

Acknowledgements
The Publishers would like to thank the following for permission to reproduce photographs: Corbis p27, (Alan Hindle) p20, (George Hall) p8 bottom, (John H Clark) p31, (Peter Turnley) p38, (Thorne Anderson) p10; Corbis/Reuters p7; Corbis Sygma (Tokyo Shimbun) p18; Defence Picture Library p54; Head AG p33; Holt Studios p14; Military Picture Library pp19, 34, 46, 29; Ministry of Defence p57; PA Photos/DPA p5; PA Photos/EPA p37; Rex Features pp21, 51, 52, (Itar-Tass) p22, (Sipa Press) p42; Science Photo Library (Colin Cuthbert) p16, (Eye of Science) p12; TRH Pictures p8 top; US Air Force pp 36, 41; The US Army/ Senior Master Sgt. Kim M. Allain p48, Spc. Jason Baker p56.

Cover photograph of soldiers reproduced with permission of Science Photo Library (Phillippe Psaila).

The publishers would like to thank Colonel J.F. Watson for his assistance in the preparation of this book.

Every effort has been made to contact copyright holders of any material reproduced in this book. Any omissions will be rectified in subsequent printings if notice is given to the Publishers.

Contents

Introduction

In the last 60 years or so, advances in weapons technology have led to huge changes in the nature of warfare. In July 1943, during World War II, U.S. and British air forces tried to damage the German war effort with huge bombing raids on the port of Hamburg. The air forces dropped thousands of tons of bombs, land mines, and incendiaries (fire bombs). The city was nearly destroyed, more than 40,000 people were killed, and many more were wounded or made homeless. But these huge raids could not knock Germany out of the war, and German industry soon recovered.

By the time of the 1991 Gulf War, things were very different. In this war the United States and a coalition of other countries went to war against Iraq after it invaded Kuwait. The coalition forces used highly technological (high-tech) weapons to reduce the Iraqis' ability to wage war, rather than killing thousands of soldiers and civilians. First, the forces used precision missiles to attack the command system of the Iraqi government and its armed forces. The missiles could destroy targets with great accuracy, even those in cities. Each one was as effective as hundreds of World War II bombs. The Iraqi forces were weakened without as many coalition soldiers having to risk their lives, and with much less loss to civilian life. By the time coalition ground troops were sent in, much of the Iraqi army had already been defeated.

Warfare today

The 1991 Gulf War was a conventional war, in which two opposing armies fought each other using large numbers of soldiers, tanks, armored vehicles, and aircraft. But today, armed forces are increasingly involved in other kinds of conflicts, such as guerrilla wars and terrorism. Modern armies are not equipped to deal with an enemy that does not engage in any form of battle. For these kinds of warfare, a different kind of fighting force is needed.

Guerrillas are small groups of independent soldiers who fight against a much bigger occupying army. They often have the support of the local population. Terrorist groups usually have political aims. As the name suggests,

These tanks are the machinery of conventional warfare. Huge convoys of military vehicles moved into Iraq at the start of the Iraq war in 2003.

terrorists try to create terror and fear through things like hijackings, kidnappings, and bomb attacks. Terrorist groups are usually small, but they are often well funded and have access to the latest equipment. Fighting terrorism is difficult. Almost anyone visiting an airport, a government building, or even a crowded café could be planning to hijack a plane, kill a member of government, or set off a bomb.

Threats and challenges

This book looks at how weapons systems and the style of warfare are changing to meet the challenges of terrorism and guerrilla warfare. It also weighs the benefits of high-tech weapons. Are the billions that rich governments spend on them worthwhile, or could the money be better used? The term weapons of mass destruction (WMD) is always in the news these days. This book discusses the threats from WMD and what is being done to try to stop them. It also looks at how new technological advances might shape the fighting forces of the future.

Changing Warfare

Like most wars throughout history, the two world wars were **conventional wars**. However, in 1945, World War II in the Pacific ended in a very unconventional way, when the United States Air Force dropped nuclear bombs on the Japanese cities of Hiroshima and Nagasaki. Japan knew that it had no defense against these weapons of mass destruction and surrendered.

After World War II came the period known as the cold war. Although there was no actual fighting between their armies, Western Europe and North America were opposed to the Soviet Union and its allies. Huge numbers of troops were sent to East and West Germany, guarding the most sensitive border between the two groups of allies.

Since the end of the Cold War in the 1980s, there has been less need for large armed forces. Armies have been downsized, and there has been a shift to more flexible, rapid-response units for use in smaller armed conflicts and to peacekeeping forces trained to work within a civilian population. Today's wars are more likely to be fought in the streets against terrorists and guerrilla forces rather than on remote battlefields. The skills and equipment required to fight an urban war are very different from those used in conventional wars. Soldiers need to be trained to cope with the demands of this role.

Guerrilla warfare

Over the last 60 years there have been a number of conflicts involving guerrilla forces. In the Vietnam War (1964–1973) between North and South Vietnam, the United States sent armed forces to support the South Vietnamese government. Despite having a larger force and better technology, the U.S. was unable to overcome the North Vietnamese, who used guerrilla tactics.

The Soviet Union had similar problems during the late 1970s when Soviet troops invaded Afghanistan and were challenged by guerrilla forces. Soviet military tactics were to carry out bombing raids followed by a huge artillery bombardment. Then the tanks would roll in. During these

After the terrorist attacks on the World Trade Center in New York on September 11, 2001, President George W. Bush declared a worldwide war on terror.

early attacks, the guerrillas retreated into the mountains, only to reappear and ambush (sneak up on) columns of troops and vehicles in narrow valleys. The Soviet forces changed tactics and started to use helicopter gunships with some success, but the guerrillas used missiles to bring down the helicopters. The war was unpopular with the Soviet people, so in 1989 the government pulled out the troops.

"We did not simply leave, we left with the war wrapped around the tracks of our tanks and the wheels of our vehicles, taking it home, and it flared up on our soil."

Russian Security Council Chief Alexander Lebed, on the Soviet withdrawal from Afghanistan in 1989

Terrorism

Terrorist groups have caused problems in many parts of the world over the last 60 years. From the 1960s onward, the Irish Republican Army (IRA) tried to overthrow British rule in Northern Ireland. In the early 1970s, the Black September group carried out many hijackings and kidnappings in support of an independent country for Palestinians. In the 1980s, al-Qaeda was set up to fight the Soviet Army when it occupied Afghanistan, and it has since become an international terrorist organization. On September 11, 2001, al-Qaeda launched a major attack on U.S. soil when terrorists flew passenger airliners into the Twin Towers of the World Trade Center in New York City and the Pentagon in Washington, D.C. Thousands of people were killed.

New tactics

Terrorist tactics include hijacking, kidnapping, and bombing targets such as airports and financial centers. Armed forces have had to develop new tactics to try to prevent terrorism. The British army gained valuable experience in Northern Ireland while fighting the IRA. It learned how to patrol urban streets, assess difficult situations, and find and defuse (unarm) bombs. This knowledge has proved valuable during peacekeeping duties in other countries.

Some conventional weapons have changed little since World War II. Modern tanks (top) look much the same as those used in World War II (bottom), although they are more powerful, faster, better armed, and better protected.

New technology

Some new weapons systems developed in the last 60 years have had a major impact on the nature of war. Probably the most important of these new types of weapon is the missile. Missiles are rockets, often with guidance systems, that carry an explosive warhead. They have changed the rules of warfare completely because they allow attacks to be carried out from a great distance away. Once it took a battleship, firing from close range, to destroy another battleship. Now a missile fired from many miles away can achieve the same result.

Two other areas of technological change have opened up completely new ways of waging warfare—satellite technology and computers. Satellites allow commanders to talk almost instantly to troops anywhere around the world, to take aerial photographs without risking aircraft, and to listen in on enemy communications. They can also provide accurate navigational information for missiles, bombs, and soldiers (see pages 28–30). The development of small, powerful computers from the 1980s onward has provided weapons with extremely accurate guidance systems. It has also made it possible to set up complex communications networks, which allow information from satellites, aircraft, and other sources to be passed between military commanders and soldiers in the field.

Weapons of mass destruction

The latest missiles and bombs are precision weapons. As well as being more accurate and deadly in destroying their target, they are supposed to reduce civilian deaths and damage to civilian areas. Weapons of mass destruction (WMD) are very different. These are weapons designed to kill large numbers of people. A WMD attack on a city or power source could completely destroy a country's ability to fight a war.

Nuclear weapons

Nuclear weapons are the most destructive WMD. They can kill large numbers of people and destroy buildings, roads, and other structures over a wide area. They also leave an area contaminated (polluted) by radioactive fallout. However, nuclear weapons are difficult to manufacture. They need complex guidance systems, triggers, and nuclear fuel such as enriched uranium or plutonium.

Biochemical weapons

Biological and chemical weapons do not have the immediate destructive power of a nuclear weapon. They are relatively simple weapons that leave buildings and other structures unharmed. Biological weapons are devices that carry disease-causing microorganisms (microbes) or toxins made by such microorganisms. Chemical weapons are dangerous chemicals that affect the skin, eyes, lungs, blood, nerves, or other organs.

Real-time TV

During World War II there was no television or satellite technology to send pictures and reports almost instantly from the battlefront. Back then, people read about the war in newspapers or listened to reports on the radio, and the news they got could be several days old. Governments often censored war reports, leaving out bad news and exaggerating the successes.

By the time of the Vietnam War, news reporting had changed. People saw TV footage of some of the action, including awful scenes of horribly wounded soldiers and injured or dead Vietnamese citizens. By the 1990s it was possible to provide live TV reporting direct from the front line, bringing the battlefield into people's living rooms.

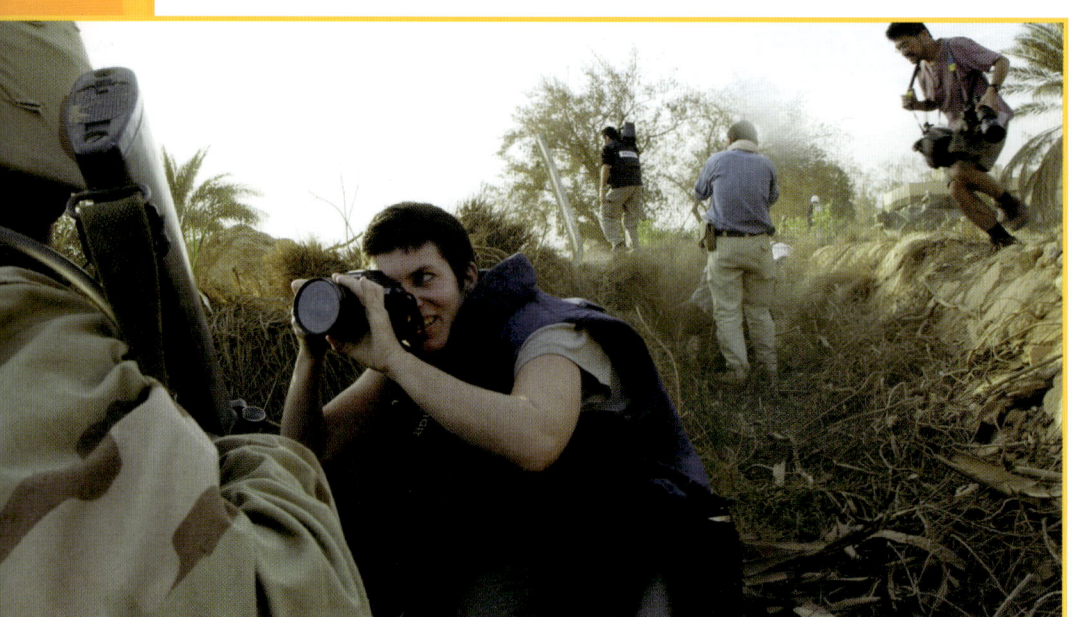

During the Iraq War in 2003, many reporters traveled with a unit of soldiers throughout the war, giving them close access to the war zone.

The change in the reporting of wars has raised many issues. The speed of modern communications makes it difficult for governments to control what is seen by the public. It is not yet clear whether such images help create more violent society or make people more aware of the dangers of warfare.

"For the first time ever in our history we not only have thousands— literally thousands—of journalists traveling with the troops, but we have broadcast media behind what I would describe as enemy lines, reporting blow-by-blow what is happening."
David Blunkett, British Home Secretary, talking about media coverage of the 2003 Iraq War

Costly wars

The cost of modern warfare is very high. The first few weeks of the Iraq War in 2003 cost the United States at least $20 billion, even though it lasted only a few weeks. The on-going cost of peacekeeping is estimated at $4 billion, and the cost of returning troops and equipment will be a further $5–7 billion. Advances in technology mean that, although weapons are more powerful and more accurate, they are also more expensive. Tomahawk missiles can cost up to $1 million each, and hundreds were fired within the first few days of the war.

Because the latest weapons are so complex and expensive, only the richest and most technologically advanced countries can benefit from them. The richest country in the world, the U.S., has by far the largest and most high-tech armed forces. The armed forces of Great Britain, France, Germany, Australia, and Japan are also technologically advanced, but much smaller than those of the U.S.

Some people question whether the costs of high-tech weapons outweigh the benefits. The money has to come from the government budget, which means that public services such as housing, education, and health care have to be cut to pay for weapons. Governments have to make difficult decisions as to whether it would be better to spend money on improving conditions for everybody at home rather than going to war.

"Every gun that is made, every warship launched, every rocket fired, signifies in the final sense a theft from those who hunger and are not fed, those who are cold and are not clothed."
President Dwight D. Eisenhower, 1953

Biochemical Weapons

Biological weapons (bioweapons) involve the release of disease-carrying microorganisms or the toxins that they produce. Chemical weapons use chemicals that harm the body. The use of bioweapons is not new. An early example of biological attack occurred in 1346, when bubonic plague infected Mongolian troops retreating from Kaffa in the Crimea (now Southern Russia). The Mongols sent the corpses of plague victims into the city using a catapult (a device with a long arm that, when released, shoots things up and into the air). In the city the disease took many lives. Survivors from Kaffa may have carried the disease back to Italy and started the Black Death epidemic (widespread disease) that killed almost a third of Europe's population.

An early chemical weapon called mustard gas was used in World War I. The 1925 Geneva Protocol (see page 18) banned the use of chemical and biological weapons, but chemical agents were still used in the war between Iran and Iraq in the 1980s. Terrorists also have used chemical weapons. In 1995 a Japanese terrorist group released the nerve agent Sarin in the Tokyo subway (see page 18).

Bioweapons

The microorganisms used as biological weapons are bacteria or viruses that cause disease or serious poisoning from the toxins they produce. A biological agent can either be released into the air, where it gets into the body by being inhaled, or it can be used to contaminate food or drinking water. Some agents can be spread by contact, after touching contaminated surfaces.

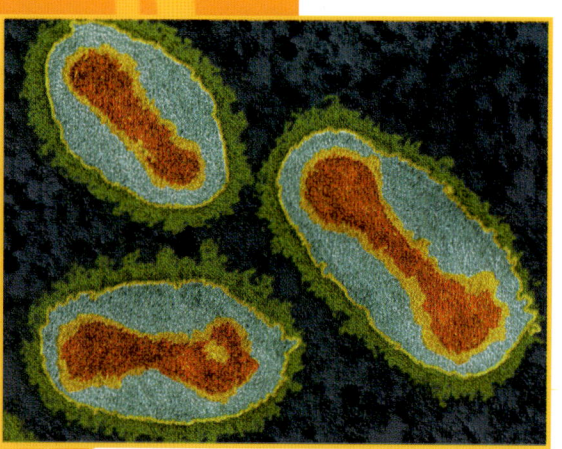

The smallpox virus, shown here, was destroyed in 1976. However, a few laboratories around the world hold stocks of the virus, and there are fears that terrorists could obtain these.

When bacteria or viruses enter the body, there is an incubation period of days or weeks before symptoms appear. During this time, the organisms continue to spread and infect people before anyone knows that a bioweapon has been released. Toxins cause illness or death within a few hours, or sometimes minutes.

What makes a biological agent?

A biological agent needs to be highly infectious (easy to catch) and deadly. It should be able to survive in the environment for a long time, and it must be possible to produce on a large scale. It is more effective if there is no vaccine or treatment for the disease.

The two most feared biological agents are anthrax and smallpox. Both are highly lethal. Four out of every five people die from anthrax if it is untreated before the onset of serious symptoms, while one in three people infected with smallpox could die. Although there are vaccines for both diseases, only a limited number of them are available.

The following table shows the effects of six biological agents classified as being the highest risk to national security (from the U.S. Centers for Disease Control and Prevention).

Agent	Symptoms	Treatment
Anthrax	Early symptoms include fever, general weakness, coughing, difficulty breathing. Death can occur within 36 hours. Not contagious.	A vaccine is available, but it is reserved for military use. If given early, antibiotics can prevent illness.
Botulinum toxin (toxin produced by bacteria *Clostridium botulinum*)	Blurred vision and difficulty in swallowing or speaking, followed by muscle paralysis. The victim suffocates and dies.	The toxin can be treated with an anti-toxin.
Pneumonic and bubonic plague	Symptoms occur within 1 to 6 days and include fever, coughing, and difficulty breathing. Death is rare.	Treated with antibiotics.
Smallpox	Fever, headache, and nausea for about 2 to 4 days. A spotty rash spreads over the body and blisters form. It is highly contagious.	A vaccination can prevent infection, but there is no effective treatment and 1 in 3 victims die.
Tularemia (rabbit fever)	One of the most infectious bacteria known. After 3 to 5 days, victims develop fever, headaches, chills. Inflammation (swelling) and bleeding of the airways causes 1 in 3 to die.	Treated with antibiotics.
Viral hemorrhagic fevers (e.g. Lassa fever and Ebola)	Symptoms (fever, aches and diarrhea) can appear from 3 days to 2 weeks. Hemorrhaging occurs from body tissues, mouth, and nose.	Some strains respond to anti-viral drugs. If left untreated, between 30 and 90 percent of victims die.

Chemical weapons

Chemical weapons are weapons that release toxic chemicals that attack the body through the lungs, skin, or digestive system. Many chemical weapons are safe in small amounts but lethal in large quantities. So chemical agents are abundant, easy to acquire, and relatively cheap.

Many modern chemical agents are designed to be absorbed through the skin. The thinner and wetter the skin, the greater the chance the agent will be absorbed, so the eyes are especially sensitive to chemical agents. The lungs are also sensitive, so many chemical agents are designed to be inhaled.

There are five categories of chemical agent. They are nerve, blister, choking, blood, and irritating agents.

Nerve agents

Nerve agents work by affecting the nerve impulses. Nerves are very important to the body. They carry information from the senses to the brain and transmit messages from the brain to the muscles. Exposure to a nerve gas leads to convulsions (violent and uncontrollable muscle contractions) followed by death when the muscles used to breathe become paralyzed. Examples of nerve agents include Sarin, a chemical that acts by direct contact with the skin, and VX gas, which is inhaled. There are antidotes that stop the effects of nerve agents, but they have to be injected immediately.

Farmers dip their sheep in organophosphate pesticides to protect them against parasites such as ticks. These sheep dips belong to the same group of chemicals as the nerve agents Sarin and VX gas.

Blister agents

Blister agents cause burning and blistering of the skin and irritation of the eyes and lungs. If the lungs are badly affected, they may fill with liquid and cause death. Symptoms can take between two and 24 hours to develop. Mustard gas is a blister agent that was widely used during World War I.

The dose of a blister agent needed to kill a person is about 50 times more than for a nerve agent, so blister agents are more likely to disable than to kill. The best treatment is to remove as much of the chemical as possible by washing, but there is no antidote.

Choking agents

Choking agents cause coughing, choking, and headaches. Liquid can collect in the lungs and cause death. Examples of choking agents include the gases phosgene and chlorine. There are no treatments or antidotes for these agents.

Blood agents

Blood agents such as hydrogen cyanide starve the body of oxygen by stopping the transfer of oxygen from red blood cells to other cells in the body. A large dose causes vomiting, convulsions, breathing difficulties, and death. There is no antidote, but injecting a sufferer with the chemical sodium thiosulphate turns the cyanide into a harmless substance that passes out in the urine.

Irritating agents

Irritating agents, such as tear gas, cause pain in the eyes, a flow of tears, and difficulty keeping the eyes open. They can irritate the mouth and nose, which leads to vomiting, but they are not usually lethal.

> "Biological or chemical agents are amenable to [can be used for] the waging of psychological warfare because of the horror and dread they can inspire. Even if the agents are not actually used, the fear of them can cause disruption, even panic."
>
> World Health Organization report on health aspects of biological and chemical weapons

Manufacturing chemical and biological weapons

The manufacture of chemical weapons uses almost the same systems and processes as the production of legal products such as pesticides. This means that industrial plants and equipment used to manufacture chemicals could be used to produce weapons of mass destruction.

Biological weapons are more difficult to produce than chemical weapons. Bacteria are usually cultured (grown) on a jelly-like substance in a covered glass dish. However, producing anthrax bacteria, for instance, is harder than simply growing a bacterial culture. The most effective bioweapon is an airborne spore (a resting form of the bacteria) that can be inhaled into the lungs. The spores have to be grown to the right size and kept from clumping together when they are released.

Viruses need to grow on other living organisms. The flu virus, for instance, is grown in chicken eggs. Smallpox is difficult to grow, and it is so deadly that it poses a very serious risk to laboratory workers that try to culture it.

A laboratory technician has to wear protective clothing and a face mask when handling disease-causing bacteria. The bacteria are cultured inside a sealed cabinet so they cannot escape into the atmosphere.

Controlling the scientists

Biological and chemical weapons are developed by scientists. In the past, several countries funded research into such weapons, and more recently, countries such as Iraq have hired scientists to carry out research designed to produce biochemical weapons. Sometimes the weapons come from research into disease, or they may be discovered by scientists researching defenses against biological or chemical attacks.

In the past it has been easy for people to get samples of bacteria and viruses. In some cases samples have disappeared from scientific laboratories, and nobody knows where they have ended up. However, since the terrorist attacks on the Twin Towers in New York in 2001, the United States and European governments have been tightening up the laws regarding research into disease-causing organisms. U.S. scientists working on certain types of bacteria, viruses, and toxins have to get security clearance from the government.

> "Doctors and other scientists have an important role in prevention. They have a duty to persuade politicians and international agencies such as the UN to take this threat [of biological weapons] seriously and to take action to prevent the production of such weapons."
>
> British Medical Association in a statement about the
> Biological Weapons Convention

Neuropharmacology

Research into the functioning of the brain has led to the development of drugs that affect the senses, emotions, and moods, and even the ways in which people control their body. This field of medicine is called neuropharmacology. Such drugs could be very useful chemical weapons. Imagine, for example, a chemical that could temporarily cause a person to lose the will to fight.

One such drug under development is 3-quinuclidinylbenzilate (BZ). This chemical causes the pupils of the eyes to widen, makes short-distance vision worse, and causes the heart to beat rapidly. At higher doses, it causes hallucinations, and the victim may go into a coma. The effects can last for up to three weeks after the poisoning.

Biochemical Warfare

In the past many countries have developed biological and chemical weapons. Some armies have even used such weapons on the battlefield—for example, during World War I and more recently in Iran and Iraq. However, since World War I there have been a number of treaties (agreements between countries) dealing with biochemical weapons. The first was the Geneva Protocol, signed in 1925, which prohibited the use of chemical or biological weapons in warfare. Another agreement, prohibiting the development, production, and stockpiling (gathering large amounts) of biological weapons, was signed in 1975. In 1993 the Chemical Weapons Convention agreed to stop the production and storage of chemical weapons.

Sarin attack

In the morning rush hour on March 20, 1995, an extreme religious group known as the Aum Supreme Truth cult carried out a chemical attack on the Tokyo subway. The nerve agent Sarin was released on three different trains. The terrorists hid the Sarin in containers, which they punctured before leaving the trains. Sarin is a colorless and odorless gas, so it is difficult to detect. The gas killed twelve people, and more than 3,000 people were admitted to the hospital. Fortunately, levels of exposure were low, and most patients were able to leave the hospital after a short time. Nine months before the Tokyo attack, the same group had spread Sarin in the city of Matsumoto, killing seven people.

Most countries have signed on to the agreements banning chemical and biological weapons, so they are unlikely to be used in a conventional war. Today, the greatest threat is that terrorist groups will use such weapons to cause widespread disease. In 1994 a natural outbreak of the plague in India resulted in hundreds of thousands of people fleeing the city of Surat. Many countries stopped flights to and from India and restricted the importation of Indian goods. An outbreak of plague caused by terrorist action would perhaps create even greater panic.

Just the possibility that terrorists might launch such an attack causes countries to spend billions of dollars to protect themselves. For example, the U.S. government has spent millions of dollars on a large stockpile of smallpox vaccines, in case terrorists were to release the smallpox virus.

Delivering the agents

Biological and chemical weapons could be released on a battlefield. Under good conditions, a Scud missile warhead filled with the nerve agent Sarin could contaminate an area of more than 220 square miles, an area about the size of the city of Chicago. If the missile were filled with botulinum toxin instead, it could contaminate an area more than sixteen times larger. However, the use of these weapons on the battlefield is risky. A change in the wind can easily carry the agent back over one's own troops and there is the possibility of contaminating a civilian population.

Scud missiles are medium-range missiles originally made in the Soviet Union in the 1960s. During the 1980s Iraq developed longer-range versions of the Scud, but they had small warheads and often broke apart in flight.

SARS

In 2002, an outbreak of a flu-like illness called SARS (severe acute respiratory syndrome) showed how easily a biological agent could spread. Although this SARS outbreak was natural, the deliberate release of a biological agent could spread in a similar way.

The SARS virus was first diagnosed in China in 2003. Over the next few months, the illness spread to more than 20 countries, infecting more than 8,000 people. Luckily, many of those infected recovered, but even so, more than 800 people died. The disease was eventually contained by isolating both people infected with SARS and those suspected of having the disease. This prevented more people from becoming infected.

SARS spread quickly because people travel widely in today's world. The outbreak caused much panic and badly affected business. Many people in Hong Kong, for example, left the territory and may have carried the virus to unaffected parts of the world. People cancelled trips to infected cities, and far fewer people took flights to Asia.

At the height of the SARS outbreak of 2003, many people in cities at risk, such as Hong Kong, began wearing protective face masks to protect them from inhalation of the SARS virus.

Without warning

Terrorists release biochemical weapons without warning, so the population is not protected. Toxins can be sprayed into closed spaces such as subways or placed in the air-conditioning systems of large buildings. Toxins can also be put into food or water supplies.

The most-feared method is an airborne attack that can spread biological or chemical toxins over a large area. A bomb or missile explosion over a city center, a crop-spraying plane, a vehicle spraying a fine mist, or small bombs released in crowded areas could all cause huge loss of life.

Effectiveness

Biological weapons are potentially much more lethal than chemical weapons. Just a few pounds of biological agent have the potential to destroy an entire population. For example, the release of 200 pounds of anthrax spores upwind of a major city could kill up to 3 million people. By contrast, it would take several tons of chemical agent to kill a few thousand people.

Most biological agents break down rapidly, while chemical agents can remain active for much longer. Anthrax is an exception to this rule because its spores can remain active in soil for years. When anthrax was tested in 1942 on Gruinard Island, Scotland, the long life of the spores made it unsafe for anyone to live there for 48 years.

Protective clothing

Soldiers at risk from a biochemical attack can put on protective anti-nuclear, biological, and chemical gear (called NBC suits) if they have enough warning. NBC suits are made from layers of treated woven fabric, used to disperse liquid, and a charcoal-based layer to provide absorption. Gases and fluids cannot get through them, and they are highly resistant to tearing. Such suits give protection against a chemical attack for at least six hours. A gas mask filters the air to protect against chemical agents, radioactive particles, bacteria, and viruses.

When wearing full NBC protection, the performance of a soldier is seriously affected. It is hard to see, hear, and breathe and very tiring to move around in the gear.

These soldiers are in full NBC suits. Although such suits provide good protection from chemical and biological weapons, they are hot and awkward to wear.

Theater attack

In October 2002, about 50 armed fighters stormed the Dubrovka theater in Moscow and took more than 700 people hostage. The fighters demanded that Russia withdraw all Russian troops from Chechnya, a province in southern Russia that was fighting to become an independent country. In exchange, the fighters would release all the hostages safely.

Russian soldiers surrounded the theater, and after three days the government sent in special forces to free the hostages. The fighters had explosives strapped to their bodies, so the special forces used a gas called Fentanyl, a fast-acting drug that causes people to lose consciousness, to put them out of action. Tragically, the gas proved to be fatal for some of the people near the places where the gas was pumped in. These people received very high doses of the gas. More than 120 hostages were killed during the siege, all but two of them by Fentanyl. Dozens more people required hospital treatment for the effects of the gas.

Until this incident, Fentanyl was thought to be a fairly safe chemical agent. Unfortunately, it is impossible to tell exactly which are non-lethal agents and which are lethal, since the lethality depends upon such things as how much gas a person is exposed to, that person's age, and his or her general state of health.

Detecting biochemical weapons

It may not take sophisticated equipment to release biochemical weapons, but it does to detect them. Currently, British troops carry two types of chemical detector paper to detect liquid chemicals. One-color detector paper changes color when it comes into contact with any harmful liquid chemical. Three-color detector paper can identify two types of nerve agent and one blister agent, each of which turns the paper a different color. Gases are detected using a more complicated device, which sucks air through tubes containing indicator chemicals.

Research is under way to develop a much more sophisticated system of sensors that will detect the presence of biological and chemical agents in the air. The sensors trap targeted chemicals, analyze them, and send a signal to a control center. The sensors could be mounted on military vehicles, creating a mobile battlefield sensor network.

Similar sensors could be used in homes, offices, and airports, just as smoke alarms are used today. They could be placed on towers, pylons, and large buildings and linked to a control center. Once an agent was detected, computers would use weather data to predict the spread of the agent and to warn populations.

A system of sensors already exists that can track the spread of insecticides and fertilizers. Trial chemical sensor networks are being placed in the subways in Boston and Washington, D.C., at the San Francisco airport, and on the docks in Miami, Florida.

"The goal for all the government efforts, perhaps three to five years out, is to deploy a highly accurate yet low-cost network of sensors that in a couple of minutes could tell you if an agent is present, in what concentration, and something about the agent. But the technology for that doesn't really exist yet."

Duane Lindner, director of the Sandia
National Laboratory, California

Nuclear Weapons

History was made during World War II on July 16, 1945, when the first nuclear bomb exploded in New Mexico. Its code name was Trinity. A few weeks later, war in the Pacific came to a sudden end when the United States detonated (blew up) two nuclear bombs over Hiroshima and Nagasaki in Japan. These two powerful bombs destroyed the cities and killed about 200,000 people.

Nuclear bombs are extremely powerful weapons. They make use of the tremendous energy that is locked up in atoms. There are two ways that nuclear energy can be released from an atom—by nuclear fusion, or by nuclear fission (see panel).

Nuclear damage

A nuclear bomb causes extreme damage. This is caused by a wave of intense heat from the explosion, the pressure from the shock wave created by the blast, and by radiation. The blast creates fine radioactive particles of dust and debris, which then fall to the ground. The degree of damage depends on the distance from the center of the bomb blast, which is called ground zero. The closer to ground zero, the more severe the destruction will be.

At ground zero, everything is immediately vaporized (destroyed) by the high temperatures. Away from ground zero, most casualties are due to burns from the heat and ultraviolet radiation, injuries from collapsing buildings, and exposure to high levels of radiation. In the short term, exposure to radiation causes severe skin burns, sickness, fatigue, and inflammation of the mouth and digestive system. In the long term, people exposed to radiation are more likely to develop cancer, and women may give birth to deformed babies.

"Atomic bombs are primarily a means for the ruthless annihilation of cities. Once they were introduced as an instrument of war it would be difficult to resist for long the temptation of putting them to such use."

Leo Szilard and 58 co-signers of a petition to the president of the United States dated July 3, 1945, about the proposed use of atomic weapons against Japan

Fission and fusion

There are two types of nuclear reaction—fission and fusion. An atom consists of a small, heavy nucleus at the center, surrounded by a cloud of much lighter, tiny electrons. The nucleus contains two kinds of particles called protons and neutrons. In a fission reaction, the nucleus of an atom is split into two smaller fragments. In a fusion reaction, two smaller atoms fuse (their nuclei join) to form a larger atom.

Fission bombs work by splitting the nuclei of plutonium. These atoms are large and unstable, and when they are split, energy is released. Fission is achieved by hitting the plutonium with fast-moving neutrons. Each nucleus that splits releases energy and more neutrons. These neutrons collide with other plutonium atoms, causing them to split, too. This sets off a chain reaction, with more and more nuclei being split. When this occurs, a large amount of energy is released, and a huge explosion results.

Nuclear fission

fission product
(or smaller nuclei)

energy

unstable plutonium
nucleus

fast-moving
neutron

neutrons

fission product
(or smaller nuclei)

Fission bombs are not as powerful as the hydrogen or thermonuclear bomb, which is a fusion bomb. In the fusion reaction, two hydrogen atoms collide (smash) at very high speeds and join to make helium. The fusion reaction requires an extremely high temperature to start, so a small fission bomb has to explode to set off the fusion bomb. A hydrogen bomb explosion creates an extremely hot zone near its center, which vaporizes just about any material and causes a destructive shock wave to travel outward.

The dirty bomb

There is great concern around the world that terrorist groups could get their hands on a small amount of nuclear fuel and turn it into a workable nuclear bomb.

Nuclear weapons are sophisticated devices that require large-scale manufacturing facilities, but it is relatively easy to make a dirty bomb, or radiological dispersion bomb. This is a bomb that consists of an explosive surrounded by radioactive material. A dirty bomb is a lot simpler and cheaper than a nuclear bomb, and it is less effective, but the detonation of such a bomb would cause great fear and panic. It would not kill many people right away, but the bomb would spread radioactive material in a dust cloud that could be carried long distances by the wind. The increased radiation exposure could kill many people over a period of years, as it increases the risk of cancer. Just the fear of radioactive contamination could terrorize a large population.

Nuclear testing

Testing is part of a nuclear weapons program. Nuclear bombs have been exploded under test conditions in the air, underwater, and underground. Since July 16, 1945, there have been more than 2,000 nuclear tests worldwide. That is about the same as one test taking place somewhere in the world every nine days. It is estimated that the total yield (the amount of energy released) from all the atmospheric nuclear weapons tests carried out is 510 megatons—the equivalent of nearly 35,000 bombs the size of the one dropped on Hiroshima.

Mini-nukes

Recent newspaper reports have indicated that the U.S. military is investigating the use of small nuclear weapons known as mini-nukes. Such weapons could be used to attack bunkers of nuclear, chemical, or biological materials buried deep underground. Even though this is just an idea, many people are already voicing their objections to new nuclear weapons of any kind being developed. The U.S. government, on the other hand, argues that it is faced with the horror of enemies using WMD and has to consider some extreme ideas to protect its population.

"The U.S. is pressing the world to get rid of nuclear weapons, yet is doing the exact opposite itself."

Ben Miller, a spokesperson for the Campaign for Nuclear Disarmament

Wherever nuclear weapons testing has taken place, environmental problems have occurred as a result. More than four tons of plutonium have been left in the ground as a result of all the underground nuclear tests that have been carried out. Another four tons of plutonium have been released into the atmosphere. Radioactivity has leaked into groundwater from underground nuclear tests, and large areas of land have been left uninhabitable (not fit for life).

In 1996 the Comprehensive Test Ban Treaty was drawn up. It does not allow any nuclear explosion, whether for weapons or peaceful purposes. However, the treaty does not become effective until it is signed by all eight nuclear nations, and this has not yet happened.

Many nuclear tests have been carried out on remote islands in the Pacific Ocean. There were over 180 test explosions at just two sites, Moruroa and Fangataufa atolls. Despite their remote location, these test explosions have caused a range of environmental and human health problems.

Smart Technology

Smart weapons are bombs, missiles, and other weapons that can find specific targets with great accuracy and even respond to changes on the battlefield. These weapons are completely changing warfare. For instance, during World War II, 650 bombs were needed to destroy a stationary target. By the 1992 Gulf War, just four smart bombs were needed to destroy a similar target. Today, as much as 80 percent of munitions used by U.S. and British forces are smart. While the use of smart weapons means that there are fewer civilian and military casualties, they cost a great deal more than conventional weapons. For example, British fighter-bombers are equipped with laser-guided smart bombs, such as the Paveway, which cost about $75,000 each.

Spotting a target

Smart weapons have sensors that pick up information about their surroundings and an information processor (a built-in computer) to interpret the information. For instance, smart artillery shells that are designed to recognize and attack tanks are equipped with magnetic sensors that can detect iron and steel. The information processor might be programmed to recognize a particular size of signal as being tank-like. It can then slightly alter the path of the shell so that it is directed toward the target signal. Shells or missiles that are guided in this way are referred to as precision guided munitions (PGM).

Smart bombs

Smart bombs have a guidance system to direct the bomb to its target. There are four types of guidance: electro-optical, infrared, global positioning system (GPS) (see panel on page 29), and laser guidance.

Laser guidance is one of the most accurate systems. A laser-guided bomb is released in the vicinity of the target at the correct height and angle. A laser beam is pointed at the target, either by the plane that dropped the bomb, by a second aircraft, or by a soldier on the ground. This creates a small spot of light on the target. The laser bomb has a moveable electronic eye that can detect this spot of light. The bomb's information processor adjusts the weapon's descent toward its target by moving tiny wings on the bomb's nose.

The main limitation of laser-guided bombs is the need for a clear line of sight from laser to target and target to bomb. In practice this means that such weapons cannot be used if it is cloudy or raining or if there is heavy smoke. Bombs that make use of the GPS do not suffer from these problems, but they do not have quite the accuracy of laser-guided weapons.

Global positioning system

The global positioning system (GPS) is a network of navigational satellites that enables a GPS user to find his or her position with great accuracy. The system uses a network of 24 satellites, orbiting at an altitude of about 12,400 miles. The satellite network is organized so that every point on Earth is within range of at least four satellites. The satellites send out a stream of digital signals that can be picked up by a GPS receiver. The receiver compares the time it takes for a signal to reach it from each of the four satellites. From this information, the receiver can calculate its position.

GPS satellites are operated by the U.S. military. They transmit two types of signal. One type is for civilian use, while the other signal is encrypted (coded) and is solely for military purposes. The difference between the two is in their accuracy. The civilian signal is normally accurate to about 52 feet, but in times of war the signal can be changed so that it is only accurate to about 328 feet. This is to prevent enemy forces from being able to benefit from the civilian GPS system.

The military GPS signal can be made more accurate than the civilian system. During the Iraq War in 2003, engineers changed the system to give military GPS receivers, such as those in precision-guided weapons, an accuracy of about ten feet.

Satellite-guided bombs

A bomb called the joint direct attack munition (JDAM) is guided by GPS. Target coordinates are normally loaded before the aircraft takes off, although the flight crew can change them themselves before the bomb is released. Once released, the bomb's GPS guides it to the target regardless of weather conditions. But GPS signals can be jammed or made unintelligible (impossible to read) by the enemy. If this happens, the JDAM has a backup inertial navigation system that it can use to reach its target. Although JDAM bombs are much cheaper than laser-guided weapons, they are not as accurate. However, they perform better in poor weather conditions.

Boosts to 1,200 feet.
Turbolan engine
takes control

GPS satellite

Payload
capable of
striking up
to 3 targets

Launched from
submarines,
cruisers, and
destroyers

Cruises as
low as 50
feet

The Tomahawk Cruise Missile

Range: approx. 700–1,000 miles. Speed: approx. 550 mph

The Tomahawk missile is a smart cruise missile that uses GPS navigation combined with a camera system for identifying targets. This makes it an extremely accurate weapon.

Missing the target

Even laser-guided missiles can miss their target. In the Iraq War in 2003, more than 8,000 precision-guided missiles were used. About ten percent of these weapons did not hit their intended target. There were many reasons for these failures, including technical and mechanical failures and human error.

Problems most often arise when targets are in urban areas, where there is a greater risk of civilian casualties. Sometimes governments set up military bases in towns and cities on purpose to make them more difficult to target. Sometimes the enemy may put out false information about the location of their bases so the wrong targets may be hit.

"No weapons system is foolproof. We'll always have one or two that go off target."

Lieutenant Commander Charles Owens, spokesperson for U.S. Central Command, discussing the use of precision-guided missiles in the 2003 Iraq War

The Apache attack helicopter is one of the most advanced helicopters in the world. It is equipped with a range of smart weapon systems, including fire-control radar. This can search for targets, decide on their importance, and use the information to control the firing of the helicopter's missiles. Not only can it do these things in almost any weather, but the radar also has a low power output, making it very hard for the enemy to detect.

Automatic target recognition

Although smart weapons have many capabilities, their ability to recognize targets without human help is still limited. A human recognizes an object through a combination of shape, pattern, and other characteristics, which the brain compares with similar objects seen in the past. Researchers are now trying to teach computers to recognize targets in the same way. However, the human brain is still much better at matching patterns and, most importantly, has much better judgment in uncertain conditions. Smart weapons have to be told what to do if they are unsure about the identity of a target. Is it a tank? A friend or enemy? Is it a vehicle carrying civilians or enemy soldiers? Programming a weapon to attack only if it is absolutely sure of its target may mean that the weapon does not work as well. On the other hand, programming weapons to attack even when they are unsure of the target could lead to many civilian casualties and troops killed by friendly fire, a term that refers to when people are killed by accident by people on the same side.

Adaptive materials

Adaptive materials are helping improve weapon design and performance. Adaptive materials have unusual characteristics. They can change shape if exposed to heat, an electric current, or an electromagnetic charge. The change in shape can be used to morph, or mold, a structure into a new shape. Wings made with adaptive materials, for example, might change shape at take-off and landing, just as a bird can change the shape of its wings. This would make it possible for aircraft to take off and land on much shorter runways.

Adaptive materials are not yet strong enough to be used for large, heavy airplane wings. They are more likely to be used initially in small unmanned vehicles, missiles, and smart weapons.

Piezoelectric materials

Piezoelectric materials are one kind of adaptive material. A piezoelectric material is one that changes shape when an electric current is passed through it. At present, the most common piezoelectric materials are quartz crystals, which vibrate when a changing electric signal is passed through them. Such crystals are used in quartz watches, microphones, small loudspeakers, and many other devices.

Other piezoelectric materials are now being developed for use in helicopter rotors. The piezoelectric materials replace mechanical parts in order to reduce vibration. In one 1997 study, adaptive materials were used to reduce the number of components in a helicopter rotor from 94 to 5. The total weight of the rotor was reduced by 8 percent, and a flight test showed that air speed was improved by 18 percent.

Piezoelectric materials in the neck of a high-tech tennis racket are stimulated when a ball hits the strings. This sends a message to the microchip in the handle, which sends a signal back and makes the neck of the racket stiffer—all in less than a millisecond. Changing the properties of the racket neck in this way gives more power to the return stroke, and cuts down on uncomfortable vibrations in the handle.

High-Tech Weapons

Smart weapons are only part of a whole new generation of weapons developed in countries such as the United States, Great Britain, and Australia. These high-tech weapons mean that fewer troops need to be put on to the battlefield. There have also been great advances in stealth technology—the art of making aircraft, ships, and road vehicles harder for the enemy to detect.

Thermobaric weapons

While smart weapons are designed for pinpoint accuracy, the fuel air explosive (FAE), or thermobaric weapon, is all about power. When it explodes, the FAE creates a huge fireball and a huge blast wave that travels at 9,800 feet per second. Such a blast can travel around corners and upward through openings between building floors.

The U.S. used thermobaric weapons against Afghan fighters in the 2002 war in Afghanistan. They were used to hit fighters hiding in caves, who were beyond the reach of traditional bombs.

Close to the blast center, temperatures can reach 4,500°F or more, and pressures can be up to 30 times normal atmospheric pressure. Such pressures can crush people to death. Thermobaric bombs are effective against soldiers, equipment, underground storage areas, communication centers, urban strong points, and even minefields. They can also be used to destroy crops or vegetation.

Mother of all bombs

There is no doubt that thermobaric weapons are highly effective, but they produce a horrific scene, as the battlefield becomes a huge fireball. They have been nicknamed the mother of all bombs, or MOAB. The power of a thermobaric weapon is about the same as that of a nuclear bomb, and some people think that they should be classed as weapons of mass destruction. Unfortunately, there are no international laws prohibiting the use of these bombs.

Blackout bombs

Modern armies rely on electricity for communications, power, and control systems. So, not surprisingly, weapons have been developed to attack electrical systems. One such weapon is the blackout bomb. These bombs release a mass of fine carbon-fiber or fiberglass filaments coated with a conductive metal film. If they are exploded near a communications vehicle, for example, the filaments touch the communication masts and short them out, causing temporary loss of communications. However, if the filaments are brushed off, communications can usually be restored. Blackout bombs can also be used to knock out power grids and disrupt civilian power supplies.

Stealth technology

The term *stealth* is usually applied to vehicles that have been specifically designed to be hard for an enemy to detect. Today there are stealth aircraft and stealth ships, and other applications are in development. Objects that are stealthy often have an unusual shape, such as the angular F117A Nighthawk stealth fighter and the smoothly rounded B2 Spirit bomber.

Difficult to detect

A common misunderstanding is that stealth vehicles are invisible to **radar** or infrared (heat) detectors. In fact, it is not possible to completely hide a large vehicle, but by using special materials and careful design, detection can be made very difficult. The engines of a stealth vehicle are designed to run cool, so that they are very hard to detect using infrared sensors. The engine intakes are partly covered, which greatly reduces the vehicle's radar signal. Parts of the aircraft are made from radar-absorbing materials, and panels are angled to send radar beams back at odd angles rather than bouncing them straight back to the radar receiver.

The key weakness of stealth aircraft and other stealth vehicles is that by day they can be seen as easily as any other vehicle. In the James Bond film *Die Another Day*, Bond's Aston Martin car is equipped with a system that projects an image of the surroundings onto the car, making it invisible. Such a system of active camouflage is actually under development in the laboratory. The idea is to create an image of the background on the skin of an aircraft or ship, making it disappear. This might be done by projecting a photograph or video onto a surface, or

The unusual angular shape of the stealth fighter means that radar beams are bounced off of it at odd angles. This means it is not picked up by the radar receiver.

by using a sort of chameleon skin system that could change color. Although the idea is quite simple, putting it into practice is far more difficult, and it will be many years before any practical active camouflage system is developed.

Depleted uranium

Most tanks use two kinds of ammunition—high-explosive and armor-piercing (AP). High-explosive rounds rely on explosive force to destroy another tank or building, but AP rounds are designed solely for destroying armored vehicles. They fire a very dense, sharply pointed rod at a very high speed, which can pierce armor. The denser the material from which the rod is made, the more easily it pierces armor. Depleted uranium (DU) is one of the densest materials known. Armor-piercing ammunition made with DU is very effective, so fewer rounds are needed to destroy an enemy armored vehicle. Fewer rounds means less money is spent. However there is a big cost to the environment and to public health. DU is a byproduct of the nuclear industry, and its dust is toxic. Exposure to just 0.00035 ounce in one week can cause health problems.

During the Gulf War in 1991, thousands of DU rounds were fired, each round creating as much as 6.8 pounds of radioactive dust. This toxic dust is insoluble (does not dissolve in water) and can remain in the ground or in the body for years. It is believed that more than 400,000 U.S. troops may have entered areas that contained DU dust.

The civilian population was probably also affected when people moved back into towns and villages contaminated by the dust. DU does not harm people right away. It can cause cancer, but it may take ten or twenty years to develop. Despite concerns about the health effects of DU, the U.S. government authorized the use of these weapons in Iraq in 2003.

Rounds of armor-piercing ammunition containing DU are shown here on the battlefield.

High-tech tanks

When you think of ceramics, you probably think of pottery. But ceramics are also used in warfare. Specially formulated ceramics can be lightweight and extremely tough. The latest U.S. tanks use a composite armor made from two layers of steel surrounding a layer of ceramic. When an explosive shell strikes the armor, the ceramic material shatters, producing an outward expansion that works against the inward force of the explosive shell.

The Russians have developed a different approach to tank protection, using a system known as explosive reactive armor. This armor is made up from bricks of explosive encased by metal plates, which sit on top of the conventional steel armor. If a shell hits the reactive armor, the explosive detonates (explodes) and forces the metal plates outward, protecting the armor beneath.

Land mines

Land mines are probably the most hated and feared weapons of recent wars because they often kill innocent civilians. Land mines and anti-personnel mines can remain active many years after a war has ended, and they are hard to detect, especially if they are made of plastic. Minefields are often unmarked, so they are difficult to identify. Every year since 2000 there have been 15,000 to 20,000 new land mine casualties. The charity organization UNICEF estimates that up to 40 percent of all land mine victims are children under the age of 15. The Ottawa Convention, a 1999 treaty banning mines, has been signed by more than 143 countries. Since then more than 34 million stockpiled anti-personnel mines have been destroyed.

Other systems are now being developed to keep people out of certain areas. The Ottawa Convention states that any replacement systems must be set off by human command rather than triggered (set off) automatically. One idea being developed in Australia is a system of pods placed in strategic positions throughout the area to be protected. Each pod would contain either sensors or ammunition and would be linked to a command center by radio. When a sensor detected a possible target, a signal would be sent to the command center to check on. This means that, if the system worked as planned, the weapons would be fired only at the right moment.

These land mine victims in Afghanistan have been fitted with new artificial legs. An estimated 24,000 people are killed or injured by land mines each year.

Non-lethal weapons

Several different kinds of non-lethal weapons are currently being developed. One class of non-lethal weapons are pain beams that create extreme pain. These weapons work by using electromagnetic energy to heat up the surface of the skin. A transmitter emits a narrow beam of radio waves, similar to those from a microwave oven. The beam gets under the surface of the skin and causes a painful sensation, similar to touching a hot light bulb. The pain beam does not cause permanent burning of the skin, although repeated exposure does leave the skin feeling tender.

Other examples of non-lethal weapons include laser dazzle weapons and infrasound. Laser dazzle weapons are laser beams designed to temporarily or permanently blind enemy soldiers from a distance. Research has also been carried out into using very low sounds (infrasound) as a weapon. Infrasound can cause people to be violently sick and have muscle spasms.

Communication and Intelligence

Ever since the earliest days of organized fighting, commanders have recognized the need for good communications with their troops and accurate intelligence about the enemy's plans. Good communications are very important because they allow commanders to find out what is happening on the battlefield and send out commands to units in the field. Intelligence is important, too, because the more military commanders can find out about what the enemy is doing, the better they can plan their defense or attack.

At the heart of both good communications and good intelligence is the rapid transmission sending of information, whether it is a request for more ammunition, an order to artillery to change the target, or a report of an enemy attack.

Unmanned spy planes

Since the invention of aircraft, one of the most important sources of intelligence for military commanders has been aerial images. During the two world wars, this information came from manned aircraft flying dangerous missions over enemy territory. The invention of satellites during the 1960s made it possible to get fairly detailed images of any part of the Earth from space, but spy planes were still important for more detail.

Today, unmanned aerial vehicles (UAVs) have, in many cases, replaced spy planes for information-gathering. They are used to fly over enemy territory and send back information. They are either remote-controlled or autonomous (self-controlled). The latest UAVs carry highly sophisticated software for controlling their sensors and weapons to defend themselves against attack.

UAVs are far more than simply radio-controlled aircraft. A recent model, the Predator UAV, weighs 4.5 tons and carries a range of equipment for collecting information. This includes radar, TV cameras, infrared, and laser systems that give it excellent night vision. It also carries a datalink, a satellite communications linking system for rapidly sending the information it gathers back to base. The Predator can fly for up to 32 hours before refuelling. It can detect and track targets and relay data back to a command post almost as it is gathered. Another form of the Predator, the hunter-killer version, can not only send back information about enemy targets, it also can attack targets and defend itself against attack with a range of missiles.

The unmanned Predator flies at altitudes of up to 26,000 feet to avoid shoulder-fired weapons.

Autonomous underwater vehicles

Most people are familiar with robot submersibles—undersea vehicles that are remotely controlled by an operator at the surface. But researchers are now working on developing autonomous underwater vehicles (AUVs) that have sufficient built-in intelligence to be able to operate fully automatically over great distances, only establishing communications with base when they need to transmit or receive information. Some AUVs will be able to navigate accurately, find their way along enemy coastlines and into harbors, detect enemy ship movements, and report back by satellite. Others will be fighting vehicles rather than intelligence-gatherers, and will be able to detect, track, and attack an enemy submarine.

"There may come a time, thanks to AUVs, when very few people are involved in violent action."
The Office of Naval Research in Arlington, Virginia

Electronic warfare

Electronic warfare (EW) is an important part of intelligence. Passive EW involves capturing enemy communications signals and analyzing them to find out what the enemy is doing. Active EW involves transmitting signals that jam enemy communications or deceive the enemy. Jamming systems can either be used offensively, to disrupt enemy communications when an attack starts, or defensively to protect your own troops—for instance, to prevent the radar tracking system of an enemy missile system from locking on to an aircraft.

Most military communications are encrypted (coded), and the codes are often hard, if not impossible, to break. But information can be gained from such messages even if they cannot be understood.

The EA-6B Prowler carries out electronic counter-measures such as jamming, enemy detection, and identification. It is armed with high-speed anti-radiation missiles (HARM) that can disable enemy radar sites.

Modern EW systems can use direction-finding equipment to calculate the location of transmitting stations. They can also analyze the type and pattern of the signals. For example, a lot of transmissions from one area may indicate the presence of a headquarters.

Deception is equally important in electronic warfare. For example, it is possible to send out dummy radio and radar transmissions to fool the enemy into thinking that they are picking up signals from a command center. Meanwhile, the real headquarters, in a different place, operates under strict radio silence.

Network-centric warfare

In modern warfare, computers are a central part of communications and information-gathering systems. Portable computer systems currently used by soldiers allow them to receive orders and information from command centers and to send back information. Communications are continually improving. Mobile phones can now be used to transmit photos and recorded sound files as well as speech and text messages.

Military planners hope that soon all the elements of a military force—command centers, soldiers, and vehicles on the ground as well as aircraft and UAVs—will be linked together by a mobile Internet. This is called network-centric warfare (NCW). It will give commanders the ability to launch air strikes or plan and control troop movements from anywhere on the battlefield. At all times they will have a complete picture of what is going on.

Networking information

Each element in the NCW network (every computer, sensor, and weapon) would publish its own capabilities and the information it holds, so that the other computers on the network can use it. Each element would also be able to get the information it needs from other parts of the network. For example, troops on the ground might want to access the latest photographs and other images of their target area from satellites and aircraft. Once they reach the target area, they will be able to add their own information about the position of friendly and hostile forces. Commanders and troops would have a better awareness of events on the battlefield, which should reduce the danger of casualties from friendly fire.

Fast Tactical Imagery

Aircraft such as the US F-14 Tomcat fighter are already equipped with video recorders that can record up to two hours of video from weapons and sensors. Pilots can also play back images, maps, and other information about their mission. In addition, a system known as Fast Tactical Imagery (FTI) allows images and target coordinates to be sent directly to or received from other aircraft and command centers while in flight. In the future, the aircraft will be able to upload even more information from anywhere on the battlefield.

Problems still to solve

Many questions still need to be addressed to create a successful NCW system. For example, how should this information be organized? Should some space on the network be reserved for important messages? What happens if there is a sudden burst of communications, such as

GPS satellite

Ground communication network

Command and control

Networking the different elements of the battlefield

Overall command and control network

Target information network (acquiring information)

Targetting systems

Targets

Radar

might occur when an attack takes place, with many units sending high-priority messages? Other issues include how to keep the network working properly when links are lost, and how to protect classified data from unauthorized use by both friends and enemies.

Disrupting the system

We have all seen how computer viruses can disrupt the flow of information on the Internet, and an NCW network could be just as vulnerable. Already there are ways to disrupt the systems that NCW will rely upon. For instance, a Russian company has developed a device that can block GPS signals from a distance of several miles. NCW is a new technology, and there are currently more questions than answers.

Perhaps the biggest vulnerability of the NCW system is the reliance on commercial satellites that are not under direct military control. In July 2002 a religious protest group managed to get control of China's key telecommunications satellites and prevented the satellite from sending out television and radio signals. If such a satellite were part of an NCW system, such an event could cause huge problems.

However, the main problem with NCW is that it is designed to work in a conventional battlefield situation. The idea needs to be adapted to be able to deal with peacekeeping operations, such as those carried out by the allied coalition troops in Afghanistan and Iraq, and for operations against terrorism and guerrilla forces.

Internet and terrorism

Technological advances are not limited to military systems. Civilian systems also benefit from advances in military technology, and this means that terrorists can take advantage of them. The Internet has given terrorists access to improved communications, systems for coding their messages, imaging systems, and global connections. Counter-terrorist organizations in Australia, Europe, and North America are aware that terrorist groups make use of the Internet in this way, and they constantly monitor the Internet to try and pick up information of possible terrorist plots.

Another possibility is that terrorists and other rogue (independent) groups could achieve some of their aims by disrupting the Internet. With so many businesses depending on the Internet, the release of a computer virus or worm causes much economic damage.

Future Soldiers

High-tech weapons may be very effective on the battlefield, but wars cannot be won with just weapons. War still depends on soldiers, and technological development is going to transform the soldier of the future.

The training of soldiers is just as important as technology. There is no point investing in smart weapon systems and mobile networks if soldiers cannot use them. Currently, it is mostly special forces such as the U.S. Green Berets that receive specialist training for guerrilla warfare, counter-terrorism, or surveillance operations to gather intelligence. However, increasingly, ordinary soldiers are trained to carry out peace-keeping and counter-insurgency operations in urban environments.

This helmet features head-up displays that include thermal imaging capability, GPS targeting and sighting, and communications links.

High-tech clothing

The separate sets of clothing (combat kit, NBC suit, and additional warm clothing) that a soldier needs weigh a lot and are hard to carry. The next generation of military clothing could change all this. Uniforms will be much lighter and made up of multiple layers. The outer layers will provide NBC and environmental protection, the middle layers will have heating and cooling ducts to keep the soldier warm but not too hot, and a inner physiological layer will monitor things like heartbeat and temperature. The suit will be powered by a fuel cell.

Helmets are likely to change, too. Within the next 25 years, it is likely that soldiers will wear helmets with a head-up display capable of showing maps, pictures, and video images—for instance, from thermal-imaging cameras (cameras that detect heat). Advanced helmets will be linked to the GPS system to show the location of friendly and enemy troops. Right now the main block to such a helmet is the lack of a lightweight and durable (tough, long-lasting) power supply.

Body armor

Soldiers wear body armor to protect themselves from injury, and for future soldiers this is likely to be improved. Body armor has to stop the forward motion of a bullet or flying shrapnel and disperse (spread out) the object's energy within a centimeter or so (before it reaches the wearer's skin).

Currently, there are two forms of body armor: hard and soft. Hard body armor is made from ceramic or metal plates. It gives excellent protection, but it is bulky and heavy and can be awkward and tiring to wear.

Soft body armor is generally more comfortable, but it does not give the same level of protection. It is made from a material called Kevlar, which is incredibly strong but light. The Kevlar is woven into a mesh. When a projectile (flying object) hits the mesh, it pulls on the interlaced strands and spreads the energy over a wide area. This is similar to what happens when a soccer ball hits a goal net. The strands that form the armor must only stretch so far, so the weave of the fibers is very tight.

Bullet-proof vests are basically soft armor, although it is possible to add hard armor plates over the top. Vests are made of many layers of strong, tightly woven fibers between layers of plastic film, and the whole thing is encased in a protective outer cover.

These soldiers are loaded down with equipment, including uniform and weapons. In the future, they may have to carry even more.

A heavy load

Today's foot soldier is required to carry large quantities of equipment, including weapons, ammunition, a flak jacket and other clothing, food and water, night-vision aids, and communication devices. In the future, the amount of equipment is likely to increase. Even though advances such as the multi-layered uniform (see page 47) will cut down on equipment weight, soldiers will probably still have a lot to carry.

Exoskeletons

So what if a soldier could be made stronger? In the future soldiers might wear an outer covering, a sort of hard shell like the exoskeleton of an insect powered by mechanical muscles. This would enable soldiers to run and jump faster and further, and to carry heavy loads for long distances.

Soldiers of the future might look like medieval knights in armor. Those knights wore such heavy armor that they had to be strapped to their horses. The armor of future soldiers will be made of much lighter materials, and motors would improve their strength to make them many times more agile and powerful. Extra strength would allow the soldier to carry additional weapon systems and sensors, which would probably be built into the exoskeleton.

Any exoskeleton would have to be strong, flexible, and capable of protecting itself and the wearer. It is likely that it would be made from advanced composites. The motors that power the skeleton would need a lightweight and compact power source that could supply power for at least 24 hours without recharging.

Staying alert

Soldiers can have the best equipment possible, but one problem that cannot be overcome with technology is soldier fatigue (tiredness). During an offensive, soldiers may be active for long periods of time, and they have to stay alert. They often have to make important decisions after many hours of activity.

To overcome fatigue, soldiers learn to grab short naps whenever they have a chance. This may be during the day rather than at night, and this disrupts their regular sleep pattern. People do not sleep as well during daylight hours, partly because of the light and the noise level and partly because of the influence of their own body clock telling them that they should be awake. Mealtimes, too, are altered. Soldiers may suffer from digestive disorders because of irregular meal times and the fact that meals may be eaten quickly. All these changes can reduce mental alertness and make mistakes more likely.

Soldiers can be prepared to deal with fatigue. During army training sessions, they are subjected to battlefield conditions so that they experience the problems of fatigue before being in a real combat situation. Sometimes soldiers can take drugs to increase their level of alertness temporarily. In the future, new drugs may be developed to help protect soldiers and keep them fit and effective. However, the body cannot keep working without rest indefinitely, so military planners must take soldier fatigue into account.

Future Battlefields

It is certain that the army of tomorrow will look quite different from that operating today. In the future, the military will be more mobile and able to react more quickly to world events. Armed forces will be able to strike more accurately and with great precision.

In the future, there will undoubtedly be more robot vehicles and other automated equipment. Artificial intelligence could enable computers to process the data and make decisions.

War on the street

Soldiers may be equipped with special equipment designed to deal with the urban environment. For example, they may have an anti-sniper system, a portable computer that can figure out the path of a bullet and follow it back to pinpoint the exact location of an enemy sniper. Non-lethal weapons will be an important part of the urban soldier's armory, too, for use in situations such as crowd control.

Hypersonic UAVs

Currently, long-range bombing missions can take up to 44 hours to complete. They may involve multiple air-to-air refuelling procedures and often have to rely on airbases in other countries. As part of the new strategy to have a more mobile armed force, the U.S. is developing a hypersonic unmanned aerial vehicle (UAV) that is capable of attacking anywhere on Earth within two hours. The program is called Falcon, and it is planned to be operational by 2025. Falcon is a remote-controlled aircraft capable of taking off from a conventional runway. It can fly in the upper atmosphere at more than five times the speed of sound and deliver six tons of precision-guided bombs or missiles on targets up to 8,700 miles away.

Falcon will be powered by a type of engine known as a scramjet. Conventional jet engines work by drawing in air, compressing it, mixing it with fuel, and then exploding it in a combustion chamber. The exhaust gases from the explosion provide the thrust that drives the aircraft along.

When it comes into use, the hypersonic vehicle Falcon could be nearly impossible to stop. No other fighter aircraft or anti-aircraft missile could fly as high or as fast.

A scramjet only begins to work at speeds of about 3,100 mph. At these speeds air is forced into the engine at supersonic speeds as the aircraft moves along. Fuel is mixed with this supersonic air and exploded to produce thrust. The scramjet will take the Falcon up to a top speed of nearly 5,600 mph.

Space warfare

Many of the latest advances in weapons and systems, such as GPS, depend on satellites for their operation. In the future it is possible that weapons systems will be placed in orbit around the Earth, and that future battles will be won by the country that dominates space. Of course, as soon as one country puts a weapon platform into space, others would feel the need to defend against that by deploying anti-satellite missiles, or even satellites designed to find and destroy orbiting weapons platforms.

Fortunately, this has not happened yet. Those military satellites that are in space today are almost all concerned with communications, navigation, or surveillance. However, this could change in the future.

Microbots

Military forces already use robots for dangerous tasks that need to be done at long range without risk to humans, such as bomb disposal and surveillance. Most of the robots in use today are relatively large and limited in their uses. However, scientists are developing tiny ground-based robots that will be just five centimeters long. They are called smart microbots, and they will be able to carry out a range of tasks, from surveillance and detecting minefields on the battlefield to checking for suspected terrorist traps. Microbots have the added bonus that several of them can work together to perform tasks that would be beyond the ability of a single complex robot.

Microbots are made from smart materials and make use of new forms of energy storage. Since a microbot is similar in size and weight to an insect, scientists have turned to biology to solve the problems of movement. Each microbot consists of a single silicon chip and a number of legs. Depending on the design, the microbot can walk, jump, climb, crawl, or slither.

Robotic insects

Scientists are also developing a range of robot aircraft known as micro air vehicles (MAVs). They will be far smaller than any conventional UAV. They will be able to operate on their own, buzzing over enemy territory and sending back information. Aircraft of this size (about six inches) would be too small to be noticed.

One prototype, called an Entomopter, is based on the design of an insect. Its body contains the power source and the fuel tank. There are two pairs of wings, with a span of six inches. The wings are made from thin film supported by stiff, yet flexible veins. Entomopter even has legs that provide extra fuel storage and help control movement in the air.

The power source for the Entomopter is a chemical muscle. As well as powering the wings, the chemical muscle provides a small amount of electricity to run sensors and communications systems. Waste gas produced by the chemical muscle is used to steer the tiny robot through the air and to run Entomopter's navigation system.
One possible use of Entomopter is in the exploration of Mars. It could be used as a scout vehicle to check out the terrain for a robot rover.

Smart dust

The development of a miniature sensor the size of a grain of rice could become a powerful tool for gathering information about enemy movements. Such sensors, known as motes, will be self-powered, undetectable, cheap, and very simple to use. Prototype motes about the size of a matchbox already exist, but future generations of mote will be small enough to float safely to the ground if dropped from an aircraft.

Motes will be intelligent and will take energy directly from their environment, probably from movement or sunlight. Different motes could be used to monitor almost anything from temperature to vibration, noise, or even gravity. Each mote would be part of a network, communicating with a few near neighbors.

Each mote will have an on-board computer. It spends 99 percent of its time asleep, so power requirements are tiny—just one thousandth of the power used by a mobile phone. Each mote processes the data from its sensor and transmits the processed information to the surrounding motes. Then the information is passed along the network to a control station. If one mote fails, the others regroup.

Phasers in the future?

On the TV program *Star Trek*, starship crews use a weapon called a phaser that can stun a person by shining a ray of light at them. Such a weapon may soon exist. A stun gun under development uses two ultraviolet laser beams to ionize the air (make it possible for the air to conduct electricity). The weapon then sends an electric pulse to the target. The electric signal that passes from the beams causes nearly all the muscles in the victim's body to lock up. The weapon would be too weak to affect the muscles of the heart and lungs, so the effects of the phaser would not be permanent.

E-bombs

When a nuclear bomb explodes, it gives off a powerful burst of radio waves that destroy electronic systems. Non-nuclear weapons that produce a similar pulse, strong enough to damage electronic systems, are now being developed. It is likely that such e-bombs will be fitted in cruise missiles in the near future.

The e-bomb emits a very brief, high-powered burst of a few microseconds in length. The energy produced can enter an electronic or electrical system through an antenna or unshielded wiring and damage electronic components even when they are not operating. Anything electrical is at risk, including radar systems, radios, GPS receivers, and computers.

The e-bombs under development by the military are sophisticated weapons, but a basic weapon could be built cheaply using simple components. This could make e-bombs attractive to terrorists who could cause considerable damage by setting off an e-bomb over a city, especially a financial center such as New York or London. The bomb could disable everything electric and electronic within several miles of the point of detonation. However, the damage would not stop with the first pulse. Over the next fifteen minutes or so, collapsing electrical systems and communications grids would create their own smaller pulses, rather like the aftershocks that follow an earthquake.

"These weapons are designed almost exclusively for destroying electronic systems. They minimize collateral damage [unnecessary, non-target damage], over-killing, and wasted effort. I tend to think this could make war more humane. So, such weapons are very attractive to governments that do not wish to be seen to use 'disproportionate force.'"

Loren Thompson, author of a recent study on directed-energy weapons

Genetic weapons

The Human Genome Project has figured out the sequence of human DNA and identified thousands of genes. As the functions of more and more genes are discovered, it becomes increasingly likely that genes will be used to develop new weapons of mass destruction. The British Medical Association (BMA) has warned that such knowledge could be used to create race-specific genetic weapons, designed to affect only particular ethnic groups. Such a weapon is a frightening thought, and it will be extremely important for future governments to make sure that information about the genome is never misused.

A much more likely genetic weapon is the use of genetic engineering to target agricultural crops. Already crop plants have been modified so that they are resistant to disease or weed-killers. In the future, crop plants could be altered so that they failed to grow properly, or so that the crop contained poisons. The world's seed stocks could become contaminated with such modified seed, meaning that populations could starve or become poisoned. This could lead to widespread hunger and even whole populations being poisoned by the food that they eat.

Looking Ahead

Modern armies are now increasingly involved in peacekeeping, fighting against guerilla forces and combatting terrorism. Today's armed forces are also spread more thinly than in the past. U.S. military forces, for instance, are deployed in dozens of countries around the world. This is very different from 30 years ago, when the bulk of the forces were concentrated in Europe. This means that the armed forces have to be mobile and able to react quickly to world events.

Both the United States and Great Britain have announced that their military forces are to be reorganized into smaller, lighter units that can be dispatched anywhere in the world at a moment's notice. There will be a greater emphasis on the role of special forces on the ground, such as the Green Berets, while the air force will be armed with more precision-guided smart bombs and the navy with more cruise missiles.

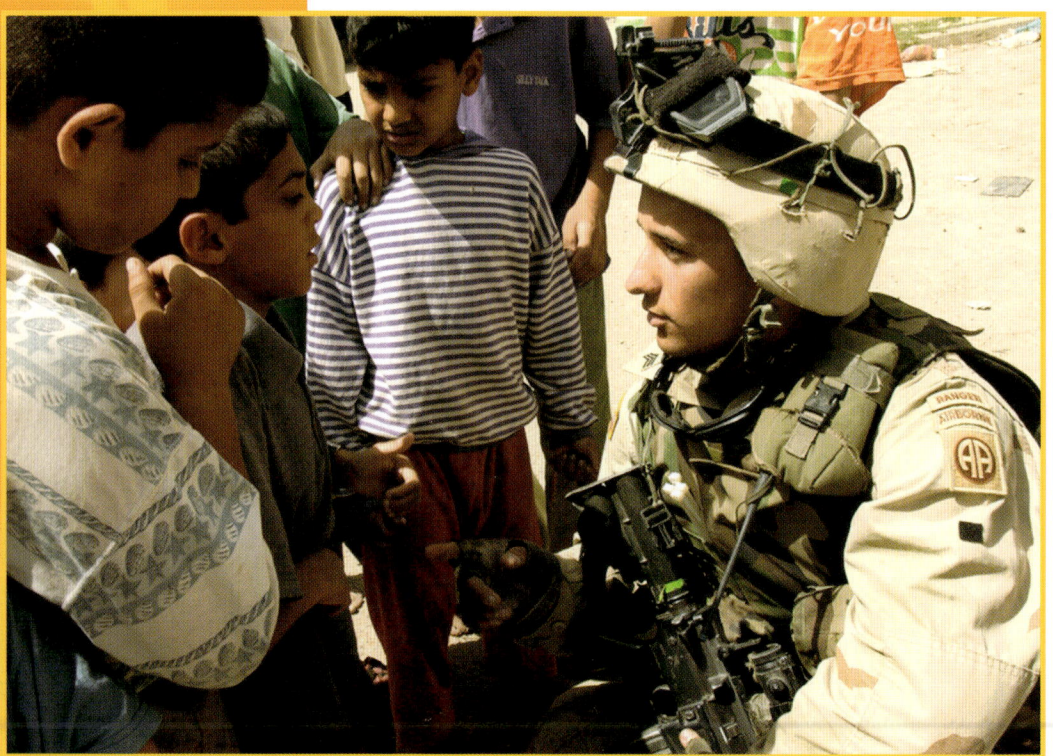

A soldier mixes with local children in Iraq while carrying out peacekeeping duties.

It is likely that the threat of chemical and biological weapons will remain. Terrorists may be tempted to use them because of the psychological (mental) damage they would have. Another possibility might be the future use of genetic engineering as a form of WMD.

With modern technology, warfare can now be monitored and controlled remotely. Here, controllers in the Combined Air Operations Center are monitoring on-going missions during the Iraq War from an air base on the Arabian Peninsula.

War at a distance

Warfare is becoming less personal and more remote. Many of tomorrow's soldiers may not even see the enemy. The number of soldiers involved in action is already lower than in the past. For example, the pinpoint accuracy of precision-guided missiles used to wipe out key installations during the Iraq war in 2003 meant that fewer troops were needed to win the war. However, this technological advantage proved to be of little or no use in winning the peace. When the role of the military changed to peacekeeping rather than warfare, more soldiers were needed on the ground to keep order and to help rebuild the damaged country.

So will wars of the future be any quicker, easier, or more humane than wars have been in the past? On one hand, the increased use of robots and automated smart weapons means that fighting can be done from afar, saving the lives of soldiers. On the other, the rise in terrorism and guerrilla warfare means that, increasingly, the role of the military is to protect civilian populations against small groups that might attack in any situation. Training armed forces to deal with both these types of future war is a difficult task.

"Another type of war, new in its intensity, ancient in its origin—war by guerrillas ... war by ambush instead of by combat, by infiltration instead of aggression, seeking victory by eroding and exhausting the enemy instead of engaging him."

President John F. Kennedy in the 1960s, talking to graduates of West Point Military Academy

Timeline

1925   Nations sign Geneva Protocol prohibiting the use of toxic gases and bacteriological methods in warfare. However, the protocol is ignored by some nations, such as Italy, which used mustard gas against Abyssinian troops in a war in 1935–36.

1939   World War II starts.

1942   Testing of anthrax on Gruinard Island, Scotland, renders the island uninhabitable for 48 years.

1944   A form of cruise missile, the V-1 or buzz bomb, is developed by Nazi Germany.

1945   First nuclear bomb, code-named Trinity, is exploded as a test on July 16 in New Mexico. On August 6, a fission bomb called Little Boy is detonated over Hiroshima, Japan.

1949   North Atlantic Treaty Organization is established, with ten European and two North American countries as members.

1952   World's first hydrogen fusion bomb is test-detonated on Elugelap Island in the Pacific.

1964   The United States enters war with North Vietnam after a North Vietnamese torpedo boat fires upon two U.S. destroyers. The U.S. and the forces of its allies (including Australia) try to fight a conventional war, but the North Vietnamese use guerrilla tactics. The U.S. uses chemical warfare to destroy the forests that are hiding enemy troops.

1968   The Irish Republican Army (IRA) uses terrorist tactics to try to end British rule in Northern Ireland.

1975   South Vietnam is invaded by North Vietnamese troops, and remaining U.S. troops are forced to withdraw.

Signing of the Convention on the Prohibition of the Development, Production, and Stockpiling of Bacteriological and Toxin Weapons takes place.

1979   Soviet forces invade Afghanistan. They are met with resistance from guerrilla fighters who successfully overcome the greater strength of the Soviet forces.

1982   Falklands War starts when Argentinian forces take over the British Falkland Islands.

1984	The IRA bombs a British hotel in an attempt to kill members of the British Conservative government during a political party conference.
1985	Nuclear Non-Proliferation Treaty is signed on July 1 by the United States, Great Britain, the Soviet Union, and 59 other countries. It is not signed by China or France.
1989	The U.S. Air Force's B2 Spirit stealth bomber flies for the first time.
1991	Operation Desert Storm (Gulf War) begins on January 16. A coalition of allied forces, led by the United States, launches a war against Iraq after Iraqi troops invade Kuwait.
1993	Chemical Weapons Convention is established. This is a multinational agreement to eliminate production and storage of chemical weapons.
1995	Terrorists carry out Sarin attack on the Tokyo subway in Japan.
1996	International community draws up the Comprehensive Test Ban Treaty which bans all forms of nuclear explosion.
1999	The Ottawa Convention, a treaty that bans the use of anti-personnel mines, comes into effect.
	A blackout bomb, released by a Nighthawk stealth fighter, is used for the first time as part of NATO strikes against Serbia.
2001	On September 11, terrorists fly two planes into the Twin Towers of the World Trade Center in New York, causing their collapse and the death of thousands of people.
	South Dakota Senator Tom Daschle receives a letter containing anthrax spores. The spores infect 25 people. Offices are closed and parts of the U.S. Postal Service shut down.
2002	A single one-ton thermobaric bomb is used for the first time in combat against fighters hiding in cave complexes in Afghanistan.
	Outbreaks of SARS in China.
	Russian troops use chemical agent to subdue Chechen fighters holding hundreds of people hostage in Moscow theater.
	North Korea admits to having a nuclear weapons program despite signing a treaty agreeing to abandon this.
2003	Iraq War starts on March 20.

Glossary

adaptive material something that changes shape when exposed to heat, electricity, or electromagnetism

antibiotic type of drug (such as penicillin) that kills or inhibits the growth of harmful bacteria

artillery heavy guns firing explosive shells and launchers firing missiles

atom one of the tiny particles that make up matter

ceramic any material that is first shaped and then hardened by heat

coalition temporary alliance of countries to fight a war

composite material in which fibers of one material are embedded in another material in order to make a stronger substance

conventional war war in which two opposing armies meet and fight each other using large numbers of soldiers, tanks, armored vehicles, and aircraft

cruise missile guided missile that uses a lifting wing and a jet propulsion system to allow sustained flight. This is usually designed to carry a large conventional or nuclear warhead many hundreds of pounds.

deoxyribonucleic acid (DNA) substance found in the nucleus of a cell that carries the genetic code

depleted uranium (DU) byproduct of the nuclear industry used in armor-piercing ammunition

enriched uranium uranium that has been processed so that it can be used as fuel for a nuclear reactor or in nuclear weapons

fermenter device for growing microbes under controlled conditions, often on a large scale

fuel cell device similar to a battery in which oxygen and hydrogen react to produce electricity

genetic engineering process by which the DNA (genetic makeup) of an organism is altered by scientists. This can be achieved by inserting a gene taken from another organism or by removing a gene.

global positioning system (GPS) system of satellites that send digital signals to Earth that are picked up by receivers and used to determine location

guerrilla member of an independent fighting force, often motivated for political reasons

head-up display display in which information is projected into the line of sight of the wearer

hijacking illegally taking control of a vehicle, such as an airplane

hypersonic speed more than five times the speed of sound

immune system body's natural defense system, which protects it against infection by disease-causing organisms

incubation period time between becoming infected with a disease and showing any symptoms

inertial navigation system navigation system that figures out its position by knowing its initial speed and direction of travel, and then using sensors to detect changes in its speed or direction

intelligence information about the enemy

jamming blocking enemy communications with interferences that make a signal unintelligible

laser instrument that creates an intense beam of light of a specific wavelength, often used in guidance systems of missiles

nanometer one billionth of a meter or one millionth of a millimeter

nerve agent chemical that interferes with the normal functioning of the nervous system, often by blocking the passage of nerve impulses along neurons

neutron uncharged particle found in the nucleus of an atom

non-lethal weapon weapon that makes a person temporarily unable to move, but does not kill

nuclear fission splitting the nucleus of an atom into smaller fragments

nuclear fusion joining two small atoms together to form one larger atom

offensive large-scale attack

pathogen organism that causes disease

plutonium dense radioactive metallic element used in some weapons

radar instrument used for detecting the direction, range, or presence of aircraft, ships, and other objects that sends out pulses of high-frequency electromagnetic waves

radiation emission of energy as electromagnetic waves

radioactive giving off radiation, caused by the splitting of atomic nuclei and the emission of small particles

radioactive fallout cloud of radioactive particles of dust and debris that falls to the ground after a nuclear explosion

satellite object placed in orbit around the Earth that sends and receives signals

sensor device designed to detect or measure certain properties such as magnetism, temperature, and pressure and to emit a signal

shrapnel fragment of metal from a bullet or bomb

simulation computer model of a process

smart computer guided or electronically controlled

stealth designed to be hard for radar and infrared sensors to detect

supersonic greater than the speed of sound

superstructure upper part of a ship, above the hull

surveillance watching a person or an area closely

terrorist person who uses violence to achieve political aims

thermobaric producing heat and pressure

thrust force that pushes an object forward

toxin poison produced by a living organism such as a bacterium

United Nations intergovernmental organization founded in 1945 that is concerned with international peace and security

vaccine substance that stimulates the body's defenses to give immunity against a particular disease

weapon of mass destruction (WMD) weapon that is either nuclear, biological, or chemical and that is designed to attack large numbers of people or property

Further Reading

Books

Payan, Gregory. *High-Tech Military Weapons: Chemical and Biological Weapons—Anthrax and Sarin.* New York: Children's Press, 2000.

Websites

The following websites give information on all aspects of high-tech warfare:

http://www.nuclearfiles.org
The website of the Nuclear Age Peace Foundation has information about nuclear energy and weapons. This site is an educational resource exploring the political, legal, and ethical challenges stemming from the existence of nuclear weapons.

http://science.howstuffworks.com
The website of the Federation of American Scientists offers good explanations of scientific technology and military weaponry.

http://www.stimson.org
This is the website of the Henry L. Stimson Center on chemical weapons history.

http://www.cbiac.apgea.army.mil/
This is the website of the Chemical and Biological Defense Information Analysis Center.

Index